INE

THE FIRST KING OF WESSEX
OF WESSEX

INE
THE FIRST KING OF WESSEX

Ray Gibbs

First published in 2000
by LLANERCH PUBLISHERS,
Felinfach.

ISBN 1 86143 083 3

KING INE

King Ine's Wessex: the background.

The Saxon invasion of middle and south-western England is often thought of as a series of set battles which saw the former inhabitants driven off or enslaved. What really happened was very different and the story of King Ine shows us a pattern of history that contrasts quite sharply with the entries given in the Saxon Chronicles which gave rise to that misunderstanding. Far from sheer military conquest, we see the unification of the two races with the rise to strength of the state of Wessex owing as much to the native Romano-British as to the incoming settlers.

King Ine himself made full use of the resources available to him as he ruled the indigenous population of his newly-acquired lands and laid the foundations of the Wessex of today. His reign saw a surge forward in church-building, using stone as the material, and this on its own indicates a rapid advance in both social organisation and the concomitant prosperity. An example of the development of social cohesiveness and control was the creation of the new See of Sherborne which allowed easier administration from the pre-existing diocese of Winchester.

Was it Glastonbury's long-established spiritual life and almost supernatural, inaccessible location down among the islands and marshes which ensured that the changes were of this perhaps unexpected progressive rather than re-volutionary kind? Certainly the Kings of Wessex held the monastery in high esteem during the following centuries, choosing, indeed, to be buried there in its sacred precincts rather than elsewhere. In protecting their church in all its manifestations they conserved their culture in the face of rebellious easterners and outside invaders alike to produce a strong, organised state. Scant though the records are it is clear that long before Alfred's time Ine, a man ahead of his own era, was achieving as much as anyone in history in just this strengthening and unifying way.

During his reign the improved availability of education allowed a cultural blossoming and the middle south-west became a fruitful source of stories of romance and mystery. The character of the region itself was a dramatic influence

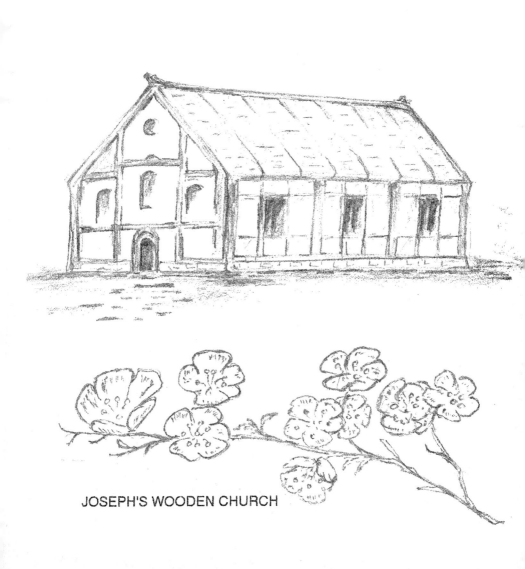

JOSEPH'S WOODEN CHURCH

upon those who wrote. Thus the literary treasures of an unique period in post-Roman Britain still arouse the curiosity and enthrall the imagination.

We have for long thought of the period following the withdrawal of the Roman Empire as the dark ages but despite our limited information it is certain that we have now to reassess the whole period and acknowledge that Ine's administration introduced a veritable age of enlightenment, of less extent, doubtless, than much later cultural developments to which we have given that name, but no less substantial. Of course, he built upon certain antecedents, for the area in which the town we now know as Glastonbury lies had for centuries been Ynysvitrin, the Celtic Isle of Glass and it was also Avalon, a name deriving from the Celtic aval, apple, the magical fruit of history. An alternative interpretation of the name is that it was the place of Avallach, father of Morgan, an ancient figure in the Celtic pantheon. Ine's predecessors, Cenwalh and Centwine, had brought the Augustinian mode of Roman Christianity to an area having not only a long pre-Christian history but a pre-existing version of Christianity itself, and they found this Celtic Church well-established, one might

3

even say well-entrenched, around Glastonbury. Thus, their new version of the religion did not uproot the established Celtic Christian ethos, already some hundreds of years old having been brought, it is said, by Joseph of Arimathea, but rather subsumed it within something new and vigorous.

The old wooden church with those legendary connections with Joseph of Arimathea was now protected in the Roman manner using lead to cover the roof. It was in all probability a Roman-style building of wattle-work on an oak frame. A mosaic floor lay within and was of polished stone in geometrical patterns of squares and circles, giving a rather Byzantine appearance. The church had long since become the centre of a spiritual life which the new arrivals influenced but did not destroy and this very early Celtic Christian foundation, set among secluded islands - for the area was then more one of lakes and slowly-meandering rivers than it now is, after a natural drop in sea level and centuries of drainage - held an aura of peace and tranquillity, but also of mystery. Cenwalh and Centwine, and a little later, Ine himself, had, despite the seeming ethereality of the watery landscape, something solid upon which to build, namely a wealth of traditions, beliefs and attitudes within the people's minds.

There were geomorphic changes too. The temporary rise in the sea level which had occurred in later Roman times wrought curious changes in the landscape and today, the change having naturally reversed, many visitors are perplexed to find the grassed-over remains of one of Europes largest fish farms and processing factories, out in the moorlands, somewhat above the present sea level. One can imagine the effect upon the viewer of Ine's time on seeing this already derelict industrial complex, left by the retreating Romans to the rising and falling tides, as it appeared and disappeared again with the waters ebb and flow. To a people who, after the departure of the Romans a couple of centuries before, had seen little of the work and development of a mature economy such a scene could only have seemed the product of a supernatural hand.

As this preview indicates, change was the chief character-istic of Ine's administration as the unification westward of an ever-larger area under organised rule gave rich rewards to those responsible and brought into being the kingdom of Wessex. In 658 Cenwalh fought at Penselwood near the present-day Alfred's Tower on the Stourton Estate with its famous lakeside gardens. At that time, by contrast, the area was known to the West Welsh as Coit Maur (a present-day equivalent would be the Welsh Coed Mawr, meaning The Great Wood), and was not merely extensive but all but impenetrable, a formidable barrier and boundary since Roman times. With parts of the area protected by water and other parts by dense woodland very few routes were available to any army wishing to cross. Cenwalh's pursuit of the West Welsh followed the ancient Hardway track down to the river Parret. Prior to this an advance had taken the Mendip Hill range to the north while, earlier still, a rapid movement had pressed along the south coast to Exeter and Crediton, but the central wetlands surrounding the Celtic Church stronghold we now call Glastonbury, even better-protected on account of having very few hardways, had remained a scarcely-penetrated buffer area.

It appears Ine was a man of mixed race like Ceadwalla before him. The Saxon suffix walla is a reference to the Brito-Welsh and the working of a certain diplomacy aiming at political power and union is, perhaps, to be inferred for in 688 Ine was chosen King by election rather than by any

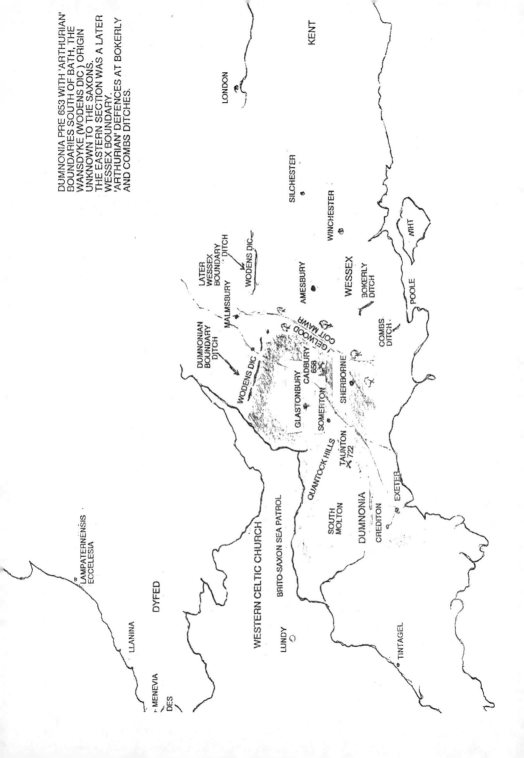

DUMNONIA PRE 653 WITH 'ARTHURIAN'
BOUNDARIES SOUTH OF BATH, THE
WANSDYKE (WODENS DIC.) ORIGIN
UNKNOWN TO THE SAXONS.
THE EASTERN SECTION WAS A LATER
WESSEX BOUNDARY.
'ARTHURIAN' DEFENCES AT BOKERLY
AND COMBS DITCHES.

KENT

LONDON

SILCHESTER

WINCHESTER

WIHT

LATER
WESSEX
BOUNDARY
DITCH

WODENS DIC

MALMSBURY

WODENS DIC

AMESBURY

WESSEX

BOKERLY
DITCH

POOLE

DUMNONIAN
BOUNDARY
DITCH

GELWOOD
COIT MAWR

WODENS DIC

COMBS
DITCH.

GLASTONBURY

CADBURY
658

SOMERTON

SHERBORNE

QUANTOCK HILLS

TAUNTON
722

SOUTH
MOLTON

DUMNONIA

CREDITON

EXETER

WESTERN CELTIC CHURCH

BRITO-SAXON SEA PATROL

LUNDY

TINTAGEL

LAMPATERNENSIS
ECCLESIA

DYFED

LLANINA

MENEVIA
DES

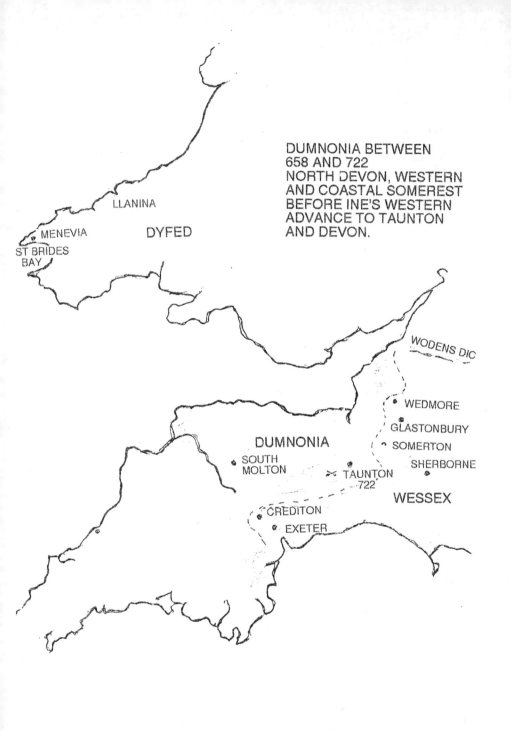

DUMNONIA BETWEEN
658 AND 722
NORTH DEVON, WESTERN
AND COASTAL SOMEREST
BEFORE INE'S WESTERN
ADVANCE TO TAUNTON
AND DEVON.

LLANINA

MENEVIA
ST BRIDES
BAY

DYFED

WODENS DIC

WEDMORE

GLASTONBURY

DUMNONIA

SOMERTON

SOUTH
MOLTON

SHERBORNE

TAUNTON
722

WESSEX

CREDITON

EXETER

kind of combat. It is perhaps conceivable that his very name suggests unity - the Welsh for one being un, pronounced like the English in. Ine's subsequent attitudes and actions certainly seem to bear out the working of a conscious aim at unification rather than of outright conquest. This view finds support in the fact that the election of Ine has been romanticised by later, medieval storytellers in a way which suggests that they thought of him as one who could unite a disparate population. It is a charming little tale, linked to Somerton, the ancient capital of Wessex.

The bishops and great men meet together in London to choose a King. They call upon God to help their deliberations and by some divine oracle they learn that they are to make King one whose name is Ina. Accordingly, men are sent forth through all districts of the land to find someone who bears this unusual name. Some go as far as Devon and Cornwall without success. Wearily, they set out to return to London. On their way back the road leads through Somerton and as they pass by they hear a churl, as he tills his field, shouting loudly for Ina to bring his father's oxen. Questioning the churl they discover that Ina is the son of his partner. Presently the young man arrives. He is tall, strong and handsome, of course . . . . . and they hail him at once as the King for whom they have been searching. They wish to take him with them immediately but his father and the neighbours will not let him go until they receive pledges that Ina will come to no harm. All this duly agreed, Ina is taken to London where the great men of the realm are assembled. Everyone is filled with admiration for him and he is chosen King and duly consecrated by the bishops.

The story continues in true medieval style with a mixture of intrigue and fanciful romance. A neighbouring king dies and his only daughter, named Adelburh in the story, being his sole heir, becomes Queen. Ina has the idea of marrying her and by so doing, uniting their two kingdoms as one state. This colourful tale has little to do with true history, but results from later additions, probably made around the time of Edward I, which show the prevailing view of Ine's place in the history of his time. In the story, Ina makes his proposals to her by messengers, but Adelburh scorns the son of a churl so he goes himself, without revealing who he is but pretending to be yet another mere messenger. He

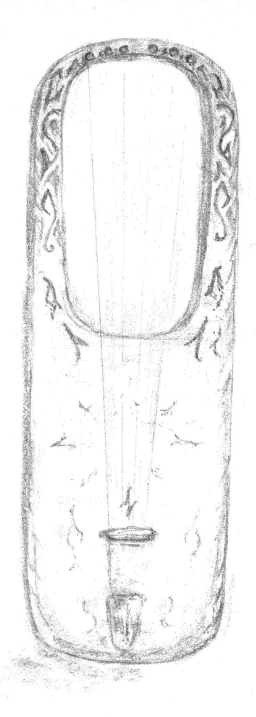

SIX STRINGED
SAXON
LYRE

stays for a while at the queen's court and one day, during a great feast, he acts as her cupbearer. His handsome looks, enhanced by his official robes, make a deep impression on Adelburh's heart. He now reveals his true identity and she is won over. He goes home and sends his messengers again, to fetch her, and this time she agrees. She returns with them and she and Ina are married at Wells.

The rarity of Ine's name and his mixed race undoubtedly contributed to his popularity, as mixed blood had also done in the case of Cenwalh. In another story Ine becomes Ivor of the British and although the historical details were in fact reversed a core of real history does remain in the records we have. The close links which existed between the west of Britain and north-western France are clearly shown and population movements from Devon as the result of plague and a mass migration to Armorica are recorded. Ancient territorial holdings are shown, with Alan as High King in Armorica, controlling these western lands.

Some of our information comes from the Annales Cambriae. These were yearly chronicles and rather brief. The Brut y Tywysogion, by contrast, provides colourful, semi-legendary accounts of events and is attributed to the chronicler Caradoc of Llancarvan. Two versions of the Brut exist.

In the earlier Brut we read, under the year 683, and after Cadwalader, Ivor, son of Alan, King of Armorica, which is called Little Britain, reigned; not as king but as a chief or prince, and he exercised government over the British for forty-eight years, and then he died, and after him Rhodri-Molwynog reigned. In the other Brut, also dated 683, we have another version of the story: Alan, King of Armorica, sent his son Ivor and his nephew Ynyr and two strong fleets to the island of Britain; and war ensued between them and the Saxons, in which they partly succeeded. Then Ivor took upon him the sovereignty of the Britons. After that the Saxons came against him with a powerful army; and in a pitched battle Ivor and the Britons put them to flight after a bloody battle, and acquired Cornwall, the Summer Country and Devonshire completely, and then Ivor erected the great monastery in the Ynys Avallen, in thanksgiving to God for His assistance against the Saxons. Following on we read: Ivor went to Rome, where he died, after maintaining the sovereignty of the Britons twenty-eight years with great

10

A SAXON CHURCH PLAN

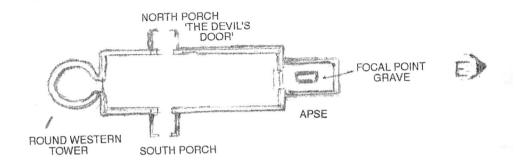

NORTH PORCH
'THE DEVIL'S DOOR'

FOCAL POINT GRAVE

APSE

ROUND WESTERN TOWER

SOUTH PORCH

GLASTONBURY ABBEY C 720

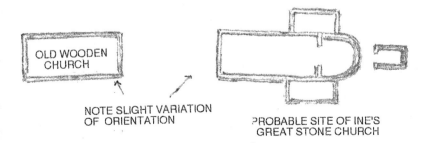

OLD WOODEN CHURCH

NOTE SLIGHT VARIATION OF ORIENTATION

PROBABLE SITE OF INE'S GREAT STONE CHURCH

praise and wisdom. He gave many lands to churches in Wales and England.

Clearly, in these stories, we see Ivor taking the place of King Ine, both being recorded as engaging in battle with the Saxons. Defence is certainly something which frequently occupied Ine in his efforts to keep the peace and integrity of his new domain and he doubtless needed the political advantage of mixed blood to unite behind him the mixed nation over which he ruled against incessant forays by their common foe from the east. But this unity would still not have been won without struggle and the early years of his reign saw him preoccupied in settling disputes between his own under-kings as they struggled for power amongst themselves. Ine was determined to succeed and by steady efforts united much of southern England as one state.

Many questions arise from the colourful but incomplete histories. Often we have but fragmentary information. For instance, we know that the ruler of the West Welsh, Geraint of Dumnonia, whom we shall meet again later, was a real, historical character, but his relationship with other recorded characters is questionable. Nevertheless we have a generally-good insight into the nature of the times.

King Ine and church-building.

During the later Roman period, and particularly from the time of Constantine, who died in 337, we see the progress of Christianity; rooms in pre-existing villas were decorated for special use as House Churches and Baptistries. Artifacts have been found and are still unearthed from time to time at sites such as Town Field, Shepton Mallet where the Christian amulet illustrated here was found. Roman mausolea, too, came to be venerated and were used to contain the remains of local Christians or Saints. Sometimes they became the focal points of communal burial grounds and, later, were incorporated into churches built on the sites. An example of such development is Wells cathedral, where King Ine himself is said to have built a church. Religion dominated almost every aspect of daily life in these centuries and, overall, its influence was positive, both socially and in the matter of education and art during a politically and militarily restless period.

AN EARLY CHURCH DESIGN
CONTEMPORANEOUS WITH KING INE

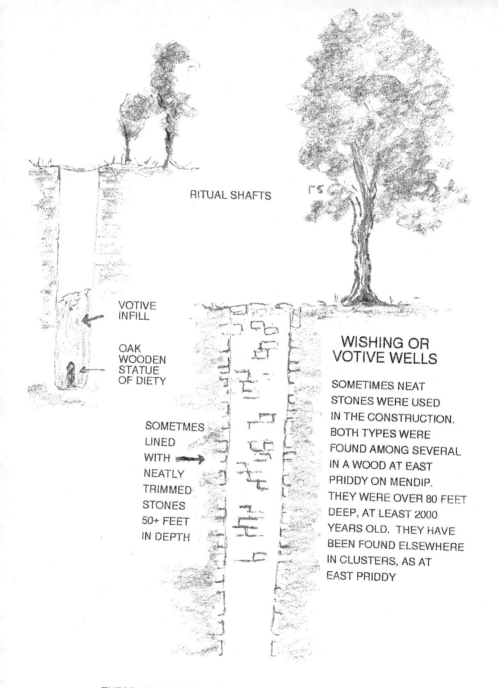

RITUAL SHAFTS

VOTIVE
INFILL

OAK
WOODEN
STATUE
OF DIETY

SOMETMES
LINED
WITH
NEATLY
TRIMMED
STONES
50+ FEET
IN DEPTH

WISHING OR VOTIVE WELLS

SOMETIMES NEAT STONES WERE USED IN THE CONSTRUCTION. BOTH TYPES WERE FOUND AMONG SEVERAL IN A WOOD AT EAST PRIDDY ON MENDIP. THEY WERE OVER 80 FEET DEEP, AT LEAST 2000 YEARS OLD. THEY HAVE BEEN FOUND ELSEWHERE IN CLUSTERS, AS AT EAST PRIDDY

THESE WELLS WERE ORIGINALLY CELTIC, BUT CONTINUED
IN USE BY THE SAXONS.

Ine embraced the ideals of the newer Roman faith but with a tolerance of the earlier Celtic Christianity, for which he had great reverence. This was natural for the south-west, Ine's own native territory, had long been the home of the Celtic Church. Missions had crossed to Ireland and Wales from places such as Malmesbury and Glastonbury. Pilgrims and other travellers passed freely to and fro. It was a church of spirituality, vigour and enthusiastic evangelism. Interestingly, in accord with the legend of the foundation of Glastonbury by Joseph of Arimathea, Celtic monks in Ireland took the name of Joseph in those centuries. Communication extended eastwards too. North-west France, as we are told in Caradoc's Brut y Tywysogion, had always been part of this cultural interchange, continuing a way of life, commerce and religion which had existed as far back as the era of Stonehenge or even earlier. It is known that those great middle-eastern navigators, the Phoenicians, had sailed as far as Britain, perhaps as early as two millennia before the time of Ine, and throughout the Iron Age ships had sailed with their cargoes along the coasts as far as what is now Turkey and beyond. Nevertheless, the way of life in the west, being its furthest extremity, continued basically undisturbed by the march of the ages which produced swifter changes on the continent. Trade with Ireland continued during Roman times and traffic increased hand-in-hand with missionary zeal well into the eighth century. Local traditions relating to this period contain a great deal of truth, though it is often obscured by later glosses. In the late sixth century St David of Menevia visited Glastonbury, one of many churchmen travelling amongst the Irish, Welsh and western British.

Defence of the coast

There are stories of Ine's maritime expeditions around the coast. These prompt us to question the tradition that King Alfred founded the navy as an organised force on the sea. The stories of Ine's involvement in such affairs lack detail but are unlikely to be totally unfounded and it seems reasonable to believe that a navy existed well before Alfred's time. Saxon naval units had been used during the Roman Empire for coastal patrols where pirate raids were common and it is unlikely that nothing of the kind existed later when the Romans had gone and raiding was still rife. The probable presence in these waters of Ine's warships should not be interpreted as indicating offensive action by

14

him against the population but rather as his providing them with necessary protection against such raiders, as Ine's own rescue after the wreck of his ship suggests, for on realising whom they had saved, the people proved friendly.

The legend is that King Ine was shipwrecked off the coast and was then rescued by the local people. The king, being very grateful, built a church on a rocky outcrop which became known as Cerrigina, meaning, in Welsh, the rock of Ina. It seems that Ine ordered that a stone church be built at Cei Bach (little quay, near LLanarth in Ceredigion) just as he had instituted such works in the newly-formed See of Sherborne. Unfortunately, like many a building over-looking the sea, it was eventually claimed by the encroaching tides. The alleged connection between King Ine and the Welsh coastal Cei Bach is just one of several which, though detail has been lost, point nonetheless to real history. Just as Llantokai, the original name of Street, the Somerset town nearest to Glastonbury, means the church of Kay so Llanina would be the church of Ina.

We mentioned Geraint of Dumnonia and remarked on the lack of detail as to his relationship with Ine. What we do know is that there was cross-border cooperation between the little kingdoms comprising what we now call Somerset and that Ine and Geraint alike respected and supported both Celtic and Roman churches. Indeed, it would be an expected obligation to defend the Christian Church with its passage of pilgrims, missions and supplies against the kind of depredations brought about in the Mediterranean by the spread of Islam to Spain.

Geraint, a descendant of Constantine (who was mentioned by Gildas, the 6th century monk chronicler) was ruler of the south-west, known as Dumnonia. His domain is shown on the map. Although referred to as King Geraint the title king does not strictly apply because the word is of Saxon origin. Ine held most of the territory towards the river Parret, but Geraint, rather puzzlingly, still had the power to make grants of land which was clearly not in Dumnonia at that time. Such arrangements seem to show how close these rulers were to each other during the early years of Ine's reign and why, in all probability, his ships did indeed sail the coastal waters in defence of the early Church. We should consider that the one route for an invader intent on taking Glastonbury and its surroundings was via the sea and the river estuaries of Dumnonia. Cooperation between the under-kings overseen by the king himself would provide the best possible protection against rebels or raiders originating from the east, whether arriving by land or sea.

Equally important was what we may call social diplomacy within the realm. Ine's laws specifically provided for the ownership of land to remain with former British owners. Equal rights were granted to all his subjects, an arrangement for which there was good political reason in view of the troubles with which his eastern under-kings beset King Ine. Marching into Kent he demanded that the men of Kent, in 694, pay a large treasure or, as one rather Biblical-sounding record has it, thirty gold coins, for their treacherous burning of Ceadwallas brother, Mul, there. Following this tragic event Ine built a large stone church at Glastonbury, east of the existing wooden church, in commemoration of Mul, and dedicated it to Saints Peter and Paul.

Ceadwalla, the bearer of a mixed Saxon-British name, as previously mentioned, had earlier acted in similar manner, erecting the old Minster of Saint Peter's at Winchester.

Ceadwalla's advance had seen the Saxons confined generally to abandoned land and clearings adjacent to British settlements. There are numerous examples of such neighbourhood development, giving substance to the policy of equality in land ownership under the early Saxon kings. It is not uncommon to find place names of both Celtic and Saxon origin attached to one location, evidence that the British remained and expanded their holdings, usually in the form of farmsteads bearing such names as worth or wick. Thus, population assimilation continued throughout King Ine's reign, something he encouraged and which led away from the risk of social strife into progress and prosperity. He oversaw plans, too, to extend church life, supporting evangelism and related secular activity and establishing regular houses as seats of devotion and learning.

St Aldhelm has been described as a nephew of King Ine. He was born in 640 and studied Roman Law, Latin verse, astronomy and arithmetic as well as becoming well-read in Scripture. Around 661 he lived with the Irish hermit Maidulf in the forest of Braden. Upon the hermit's death circa 675 Aldhelm became Abbot of a monastery at a place which, in time, became known as Malmesbury. For over thirty years he worked hard as a missionary in Selwood, the former Coit Maur of Roman times which we mentioned earlier.

Hedde had been bishop at Winchester for twenty-seven years, though during his tenure there were suggestions that the See be divided. It was decided to leave the matter until Hedde's death, which occurred in 703, and in 706, under Ine, the new Diocese of Sherborne was created, though in those early years it was known as Selwoodshire. It was Aldhelm who became the first Abbot there and it is known that he worked closely with Ine, not only acting as counsellor to the king but enthusiastically forwarding the establishment of churches and religious settlements. Aldhelm was an exponent of Roman Christianity as opposed to the earlier Celtic-Byzantine religion, and wrote pressuring letters to Geraint of Dumnonia who, like Ine, strove rather to respect each church equally. However, Geraint made land grants to the new See of Sherborne, as did Ine with his building works at Celtic Glastonbury where he built the stone Abbey Church of Saints Peter and Paul.

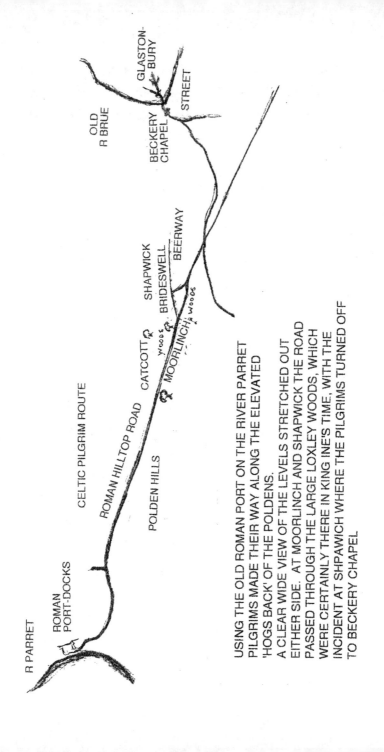

R PARRET

ROMAN
PORT-DOCKS

CELTIC PILGRIM ROUTE

ROMAN HILLTOP ROAD

POLDEN HILLS

CATCOTT

SHAPWICK

BRIDESWELL

BEERWAY

MOORLINCH

OLD
R BRUE

BECKERY
CHAPEL

GLASTON-
BURY

STREET

USING THE OLD ROMAN PORT ON THE RIVER PARRET
PILGRIMS MADE THEIR WAY ALONG THE ELEVATED
'HOGS BACK' OF THE POLDENS.
A CLEAR WIDE VIEW OF THE LEVELS STRETCHED OUT
EITHER SIDE. AT MOORLINCH AND SHAPWICK THE ROAD
PASSED THROUGH THE LARGE LOXLEY WOODS, WHICH
WERE CERTAINLY THERE IN KING INE'S TIME, WITH THE
INCIDENT AT SHPAWICH WHERE THE PILGRIMS TURNED OFF
TO BECKERY CHAPEL

...BY A SHAFT OF LIGHT TO A WELL

Communications between the early churches and the civil rulers were close. Moreover, these were busy and prosperous years, with advances in agriculture and artistic achievement in book decoration, particularly in the Winchester Style which matched or surpassed the work of the rest of Europe. But all was not entirely peaceful. Rivalry between the two versions of Christianity manifested itself in the establishment of a monastery at Wells which was alleged to have been brought into being specifically to control Glastonbury with its associated hermitages and chapels occupying the inaccessible islands of the central Somerset wetlands. There is evidence of friction between the two churches in the story of Ine's search for two Irish pilgrims who had in fact been killed at Shapwick Woods while visiting Glastonbury Abbey. The route taken by the pilgrims, the old Roman road between Glastonbury and the river Parret, lay in the Celtic border area. King Ine, it is said, discovered the victims bodies in a well, being directed there by a shaft of light over it. The bodies were, appropriately, placed in the original Celtic wooden church.

Land grants show that even Glastonbury lost lands at Brent

Knoll for a while as Saxon-Roman influence made gains at the expense of the Abbey. With King Ine's patronage, Aldhelm founded churches at Frome and at Bradford-on-Avon, then known by the Saxon name of Wirtgenesburg. The Saxon church there still stands today. Wells, with its clerics placed so ominously close to Glastonbury, was doubtless typical of the new settlements of the time. By later standards they were small, but they were more numerous than is usually appreciated.

Alongside the establishment of new settlements there were changes in those built earlier. The Romans had gone and their legacy of large houses had fallen successively into Brito-Welsh and Saxon hands. The change was not merely one of ownership. As society became more organised, along the two distinct but interacting axes of Church and State, the very nature of ownership of these more substantial, more permanent and, naturally, more desirable former Roman properties also changed. The common people lacked the architectural technology to make use of these substantial buildings. It was natural that they should fall into ruins or be taken over either by the secular rulers or by the Church. The Church, which is to say the later

21

Roman Church rather than the Celtic, was becoming powerful and did so in part by increasing its holdings in formerly-Roman real estate.

Thus, if we look, for example, into the early times of the Manor of Wedmore it can be clearly seen that following Roman occupation it became a property of the Church. Later, of course, it became very much involved with King Alfred and the rise of Royal Wessex. The first Saxon church at Wedmore, built of stone, had a large western round tower which was pulled down, eventually, for building material, in the seventeenth century. Such a building was typical of the period of the Church's vigorous expansion in Ine's time and it would have had, at that time, a number of monks or clerics in its service.

Another building of Ine's period stood on the Glastonbury site of Beckery, a basilican chapel with walls of up to three feet in thickness and, overall, similar to Aldhelm's church at Bradford-on-Avon. The Beckery island settlement is strongly linked by tradition with visits by Irish pilgrims, a view which seems well-supported by the story of King Ine's concern for the fate of the two unfortunate pilgrims visiting

SAXON COPIES
OF LATE ROMAN COINS.
DEGENERATE DESIGNS.

7-8c. SAXON PENNY PIECES

A LATER PENNY

SAXON MONASTIC
ARTWORK

INSIDE VIEW OF AN 8c. SAXON CHURCH.
THE NORTH DOOR BECAME KNOWN AS THE DEVIL'S DOOR,
AND CONSEQUENTLY THE SOUTH DOOR WAS MOSTLY USED.

AN EARLY SAXON CHURCH WITH A ROUND TOWER

via Shapwick.

The Glastonbury monastic area, recorded later as the XII Hides, was situated amidst marshes and made use of substantial Roman buildings which stood on small, isolated islands. Such an establishment, encompassed by nature itself with water, did not need the safety of a monasterii vallum, the artificial ditch surrounding many early settlements including Glastonbury itself.

The XII Hides mentions the islands of Beckery, Marchey, Barrow, Meare, Godney and Nyland, and not many miles away was Brent Knoll. All these, through their physical isolation and their Celtic heritage, remained beyond Saxon control for nearly a century. The various artifacts found at these sites show the value placed upon their natural security for they give clear evidence of continuous occupation from pre-Roman times to the present.

During 709 Aldhelm, living at the time on the western side of the Great Forest, asked to be carried to the wooden church at Doulting, on the higher ground beyond the wetlands, where he died. The church there is dedicated to

SAXON
POTTERY

SAXON
GLASSWARE

his memory as Saint Aldhelm. From Doulting his body was carried seven miles each day, with crosses built at each resting place, until the cortege reached Malmesbury. He was succeeded at Sherborne by Bishop Forther who was another benefactor to Glastonbury, giving the inland waterway harbour and land at Bleadney, a little north of Glastonbury, in 712.

Technological advance

Like any other organisation, the Church needed economic support and improving technology allowed the necessary profitable economy to come into being. One of the most important power sources was the water mill. A few mills had been set up by the Romans and, according to the surrounding terrain and volume of flow, were usually of undershot or overshot design. These words refer, respectively, to the water passing underneath the wheel or, via a chute at a higher level, over the top of the wheel and so downwards onto the paddles on the far side of the wheel. The motion from the horizontal shaft or axle of the waterwheel itself was transferred to the vertical grinding shaft by means of pegged wheels set at right angles to form a crude version of todays crownwheel and pinion or bevel gears. To avoid the complication of having to translate motion around a horizontal axle to motion around a vertical one a simpler mill could be set up with the wheel lying on its side, almost on the bed of the watercourse, or race as it is called. Such a wheel is described as breast-shot and it turned a single vertical shaft which drove directly the grinding stones on the floor above without need of pegged gearwheels. These breast-shot mills were not the most powerful since they neither used the weight of the water to turn the wheel, as did the overshot wheel, nor could they trap the energy of the water flow as efficiently as a well-arranged undershot wheel and for these reasons they were eventually superseded. Today, their presence in former times can only be inferred from the shape or layout of the remaining watercourse. A lost example may have stood in the river Axe, near Monks Ford at Wookey. Excavated Saxon mill sites from this period have shown them to have had leaded glass windows and quite refined ironwork within.

An economy resulting from a technology which extended to power milling was strong enough to support the vigorous

25

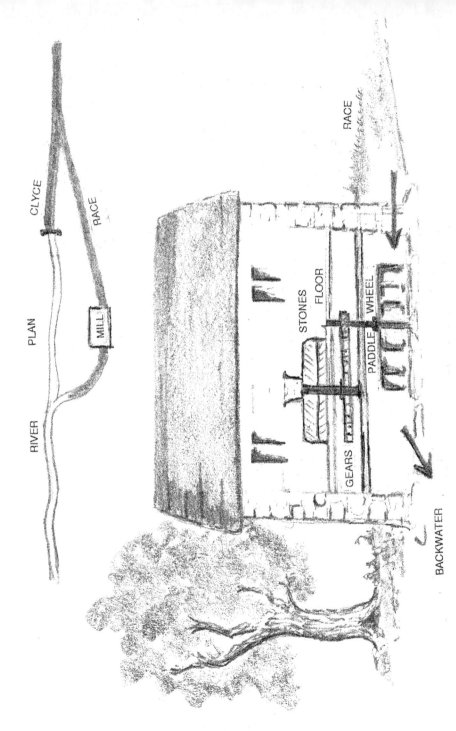

PLAN

RIVER

CLYCE

RACE

MILL

STONES

FLOOR

GEARS

PADDLE WHEEL

RACE

BACKWATER

AN EARLY WATER MILL. BREAST TYPE

church-building we have noted. Only by contemplation of such countryside developments do we perceive something not directly remarked in the records of King Ine, the hand-in-hand progress of technology and social administration which, together, produced an age of expansion. Some of the early land grants and charters belonging to Glastonbury Abbey provide us with further background information. There has been much criticism of these Charters by historians, but their details, seen through the eye of those familiar with the locations concerned, have the authentic quality of place and time. The Charter of 712 concerning Bleadney harbour sets out for us the pattern of administration for almost the whole of the Somerset wetlands. Simple deductions can be tested by research aimed to discover remaining vestiges of Ine's period. As an example, there are extensive silt formations which show the course of an Abbey canal system from the river Axe at a place called Scotland to one of its islands at Barrow. From this the water level, land availability, existence of fisheries etc., can all be inferred or observed, even the size of the remaining raised peat beds in the moors around show clearly the extent of marine intrusion.

Another Charter, dating from a little later, shows another lost estate of the Abbey and with it the land development and changes in ownership which began in Ine's reign. The small estates of late Roman and early Saxon owners began to be re-organised by various Deeds of Gift into quite vast estates. Near Wookey is a manor known by the Saxon name of Worth. In Celtic times it had the name Oar. Its origins may lie in an Iron Age land division having connections with the crouched burial found there in an orchard.

The mixture of Saxon and Celtic names has produced mystery and confusion. The river crossing and ancient woodsite known as Monks Ford and Monks Wood being so close to the Bishops Manor at Wookey and having eventually been absorbed into it, scholars thought that there had been a priory on the site at one time, but an Abbey Charter sometimes considered false on account of difficulties in identifying the property concerned now explains the situation. Comprising no more than a manor house, some cottages and, possibly, a Norse type mill, the manor came into the ownership of Glastonbury with a gift by Abbess Bugga in 820 as Oara - the original Celtic title.

Notes to Map

History very often turns out to be as a series of heroic battles and dramas of one sort or another but if a study is taken of developments in the countryside as a whole, the definition of events become so much more vivid.

During King Ine's reign the population looked back to the past as a lost age of achievement. The map shows how time, tide, mortality and economic breakdown, left a ghostly trail of landscape features, that tell you of bygone times very different than the one presented to-day.

Laid out quite differently, these divisions reflect the limits and progress of lost ages.

The 18 and 19c grid of the last enclosures of the common lands cut through a system that had all been long forgotten. A field presently occupied by Mr. Millard on Knowle Moor, splendidly retains the vestiges of ditches and clay walls.

A 14c Manorial enclosure ditch shows abandoned areas of commons. Field roadways where there for uses belonging to those early times. Plough teams used them, ritual boundary walks regularly paced them out between tenant and sub-tenant who's holding owed much to King Ine's time, the Roman and the Bronze ages.

Parish boundaries, deeply incised lanes, some field hedges and even old cottage gardens can have their origins dating as far back as the Bronze Age.

During the reign of King Ine there was an abundance of small estates in the countryside, many of which owed their existence to the Roman administration.

To give some examples, the adjoining map shows around seven holdings of sub-tenants subject to the two Tenants in chief, namely the Wells Bishops and the Glastonbury Abbots.

Looking closely, we can see where the Roman estate was partially abandoned during the medieval period and became common land served by a wooden cattle bridge over the later 14c manor enclosure ditch.

Two cattle warden houses sites are shown, one near the bridge crossing point and along the ancient manorial bounds roadway know as the Broadway Way. Unfortunately late 20c parish politics together with a disrespect for original footpath routes has led to these ancient routes and boundaries being distorted or closed. Contrasting sharply with events in the 15 and 16 centuries where a William Tucker was fined heavily at the Wookey Court for obstructing the common way across the fields at Broadmead from Ford Lane!

Some sections of the economy survive whatever else is going on. The Mendip lead mines had been worked from early times, but the Romans had turned them into a major company to recover the valued resource.

Of course, by King Ine's reign operations would have been considerably reduced. Nevertheless the enterprise continued, for a medieval record reports that the Wells' bishop was advised to transport the lead ore to his Wookey manor for smelting there, because of the risk of theft.

Traces of this arrangement still linger on in an old site near the river Axe call "Cinderford" the original name of Longwater, and in fields named "Blackpool".

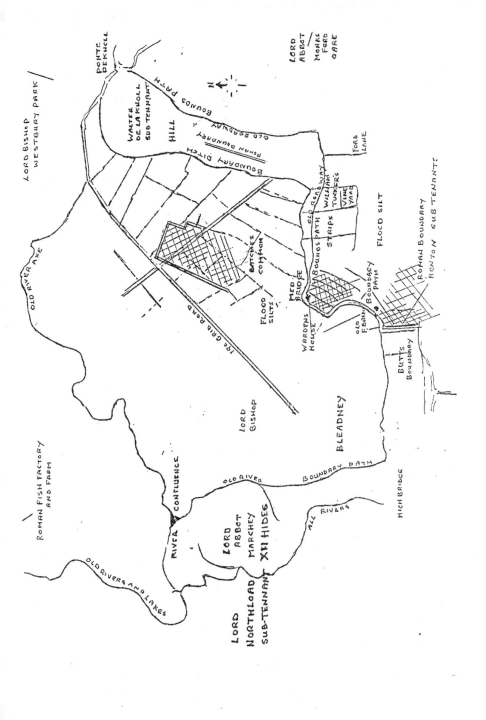

Today, a number of fields there still carry that original title, showing the value of contemporary local knowledge in solving some of the puzzles of the past.

With such extant examples in our minds we can better imagine the living realities of King Ine's reorganisations. The past becomes alive with the drama of events and we see the present-day countryside, our heritage, with new eyes.

Ine moves westward

Having subdued unrest in the eastern areas of his realm King Ine began a western expansion. Growing intolerance on the part of the Roman Church towards its Celtic-Byzantine sister may have added impulse to this movement west. Small missions and monasteries had become better organised with the founding of the See of Sherborne and Ine's statesmanlike qualities saw him presiding over and advising the first Saxon Synods. A parallel westward political expansion by military means was to be expected.

His election as King had brought a certain amount of

rivalry but he had carefully strengthened his position as Bretwald or Overking in the west. Some land earlier won from the British by Cealwin in the Severn valley to the north, around Bath, had been lost to the kingdom of Mercia, so Ine seems to have decided that he would be better employed with efforts to consolidate the rest of Somerset and Devon rather than challenging the established kingdom of Mercia. One of his first objectives in Somerset would be to gain its remaining coastal regions, around the rivers Axe and Brue, land which was in fact part of Geraint's Dumnonia.

Looking at todays maps will not give much help in perceiving what was involved. There have been variations in both climate and geology in the region since the time of Ine. A better impression is gained by viewing the landscape itself, when the observer more easily imagines the wet state of most of this area in Ine's time. During the seventh and eighth centuries a large part of what is now known as the Somerset Levels was estuary flats, silt embankments and marshes. Brent Marsh was an area of large river meanders traversing an area entirely flat apart from a few islands and even today the medieval river

Siegar is visible when its course floods in very wet conditions. One begins to grasp the task of Ine when one realises that, at his time, no fewer than seven rivers flowed slowly across the area towards the sea and frequently flooded vast expanses of the flat, low surrounding country which, at the driest of times, was in places scarcely more solid than marsh. The marine transgression of Roman times had seen these seven rivers backing up and overspreading their existing banks as far inland as Pilton and Wookey. Villas, farms, even factories were drowned out. Along the coastal area a large mud flat, several miles wide, buried Roman sites with up to five feet of estuary mud. The only areas of usable land remaining were islands such as Brent Knoll, Pawlett and Glastonbury. Such difficult conditions meant that the coastal settlements remained within Geraint's kingdom of Dumnonia for some considerable time.

Centwine, before Ine's time, had followed the land ridge down into the island of Wedmore and, taking possession of it, had offered it to Wilfrid, Bishop of York, no doubt thinking a monastery would be built there, but Ceadwalla, his successor, would not confirm Wilfrid's transfer of

Wedmore to Glastonbury and kept it instead as his own royal island.

Brent Knoll island, another property of the Abbey, was cut off and lost to the Dumnonians for some time. King Ine's advance westward then restored Brent to Abbot Beorhtwald, third Saxon abbot of the monastery. Land grants again followed Ine's advance onto the Polden Hill range further down the Levels. This and Ine's building of a new stone church at the abbey put Glastonbury in a dominant position among the Somerset marshlands. Consolidation continued with the taking of Zoy Island (Sowy), which became yet another royal gift to the Abbey.

With Kent and the London region under firm control, Ine had Nunna, an under-king of Sussex (who has been described as Ines kinsman) join him in an attack upon Geraint at Langport in 710. Even with all the forces they could muster, the Saxons began to lose the battle. Geraint, who commanded a region from Dyfed to Cornwall and had links with Armorica, proved a very able opponent. However, Ine and Nunna were eventually victorious. Some think Centwine had reached Cructan (Creech Barrow)

31

LATER SAXON BUILDING

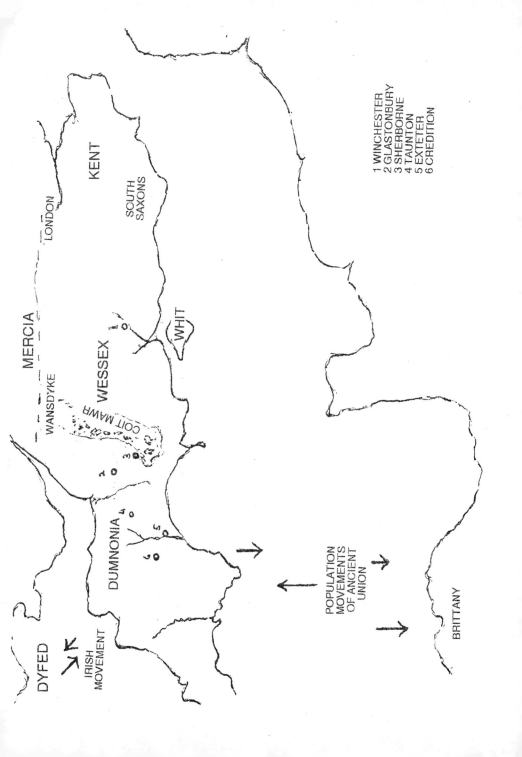

MERCIA

LONDON

KENT

SOUTH
SAXONS

WANSDYKE

WESSEX

COIT MAWR

WHIT

DYFED

IRISH
MOVEMENT

DUMNONIA

POPULATION
MOVEMENTS
OF ANCIENT
UNION

BRITTANY

1 WINCHESTER
2 GLASTONBURY
3 SHERBORNE
4 TAUNTON
5 EXTETER
6 CREDITION

earlier, but of Ine's successful advance there is no doubt despite uncertainties as to the siting of his fortress there. After Ine's victory over Geraint a strong fortress was constructed at Taunton.

Somerset saw a generally-peaceful integration between the indigenous Britons and the long-present Celts with the newly-arriving Saxon immigrants and the different groups lived in close proximity and began to intermarry. Recent DNA tests show families still living on the same farm holdings today as their Iron Age ancestors of two and a half thousand years ago. By contrast, Devon had seen the mass migration over to Armorica mentioned earlier. The reasons put forward suggest the ravages of plague as the cause, but from ancient times there appear to have been periods of folk movement back and forth across the Channel, not all to be so explained. And other movements also took place. Exeter had long seen Saxon occupation by seafarers travelling along the south coast. Interestingly, the city appears to have accommodated both Celtic and Roman churches. Escanceaster, as it was then known, had a monastery at which Wynfrith, later named Saint Boniface, first studied as a boy. As at Glestingaburg (Glastonbury),

HOT CROSS BUN / SAXON BUN

ORIGINALLY EACH QUARTER REPRESENTED
EACH SEASON, BEING WINTER, SPRING, SUMMER,
AUTUMN. IT WAS ADOPTED BY THE CHURCH AS A
CROSS SYMBOL.. ITS USE ALMOST CEASED DURING
THE SEVENTEENTH CENTURY, BUT IT WAS LATER
RESTORED FOR EASTER.

the Church still showed the influence of the Celtic fervour of its earlier teachers. Boniface, born at Crediton in 675, became a great missionary to Germany and became Archbishop of Mainz. Most of the Saxon monks and clerics were less energetic. Examination of the structure of bones from an ossary revealed that almost every one of them was very obese. It seems that under King Ine a time of plenty and prosperity was enjoyed - by churchmen at least.

Another overview, and further events

Power struggles amongst the Saxon kingdoms again saw the Mercian king, Ceolred, trying his luck by an attack upon Wessex at Wodnesbeorge, probably near present-day Swindon, in 715. Little is recorded about the battle but it would appear that Ine's army gave Ceolred the better idea of returning home. The Chronicles record that in 722 Ine's queen, Aethelburh, destroyed Taunton (Tantun), which he had himself built earlier. This might seem a colourful elaboration by history-makers but, following on, we read that Ealdbriht the Exile went into Surrey and Sussex. Three years later, Ine put down a rebellion there and slew the Aetheling Ealdbriht who had been driven out. It seems, therefore, that Ealdbriht had tried to oust King Ine by attempting a rebellion at Taunton, failing in which he had returned to Surrey to stir up further rebellion there.

Overall, the Saxons had, by their in-fighting, been a source of continual trouble to Ine whilst his British subjects in the west had accorded him respect. The reason for such perhaps unexpected behaviour may well have been Ine's origin, for, like Ceadwalla before him, he was of mixed race. For this very reason other members of the Saxon dynasty had doubtless felt they had a better right than he to the throne. By contrast with their mentality, that of the ruthless conqueror, Ine's policy was to introduce a series of codes and laws in which the British had equal rights of property ownership and individual rights allowing pro-motion to high office which saw them serving as councillors on the king's comitatus. Laws such as these, which left hereditary landowners undisturbed and gave opportunity for advancement in public life for others brought him loyalty and respect. A strong leader, who could be tough and uncompromising when necessary yet one who encouraged the best from his extending kingdom in the west, King Ine was well ahead of his time and earned the respect of ensuing centuries.

Ine's later years

For those who could afford it, to make a pilgrimage to Rome in their final days and be baptised by the Pope was the ultimate aim of life. Ines predecessor, Ceadwalla, had, in 688, done just that, and in 726 Ine abdicated in favour of Aethelheard in order to make his own journey to Rome. Several factors influenced his decision to leave his kingdom and to live in Rome. The devout faith of his Queen, Aethelburh, is generally overlooked, but her influence on the King should be taken into consideration. We may highlight this with the charming little story which tells of her method of changing Ine's mind on the matter, but before we re-tell that legend let us look back and assess what had been accomplished. Despite being frequently so described, Ine was not the conqueror of the Western British. Rather, his military success lay in his ability to control his rebellious Saxon rivals and his enduring fame and, indeed, his greatness arose out of his skilful administration of the emerging state of Wessex.

Ine's relationship with Geraint had, for most of the time, appeared amicable but his drive westward may well have been encouraged by the growing intolerance of the Roman Church towards its elder Celtic-Byzantine sister. The population vacuum in Devon caused by the plague had certainly played a significant part in the establishment of his growing kingdom, but the further moves into Cornwall had seen that impetus fail rapidly. The eighth century as a whole saw Church prosperity grow to one of its highest peaks and Ine had led the way forward in reforms and in the organisation and endowment of property, particularly in central Somerset. Women, too, had achieved greater equality and power than they were to do for some centuries afterwards and, as if symbolic of that status, the story of Aethelburh's persuasion of Ine to abdicate and live in Rome may contain a greater proportion of truth than might at first be suspected.

Queen Aethelburh's ideals were clearly informed by her religious convictions. Family power disputes and a reluctance to see the defeat of Geraint, benefactor to Ine's own new church at Sherborne and himself a popular ruler and figurehead for both races, had very likely brought dismay at such earthly behaviour to a queen whose thoughts turned ever more towards higher matters. After very extravagantly feasting his nobles and court one day Ine left his palace to reside at another manor house, accompanied by Aethelburh. Unknown to him, she had, before leaving, given instructions to the stewards to vandalise the palace, hide its treasure, put rubbish in it and let a sow and litter of piglets loose in the kings bed. Before they had gone far the queen asked Ine to return and after showing him around the terrible mess in the palace asked him to consider the vanity of earthly pomp. Thus she persuaded the king to lay aside his crown and make a pilgrimage with her to the city of Rome. In Rome, they lived as ordinary people for the remainder of Ine's life, endowing a school where Anglo-Saxon children could receive a wider education on a par with that given to children from other countries who were living in the city. Upon Ine's death Queen Aethelburh returned to Wessex and died there herself, in a monastery.

Saxon Names

Colwyrhta	Charcoal Burner
Preost	Priest
Crocwyrhta	Potter
Fiscere	Fisherman
Stanwyrhta	Stone Mason
Treowyrhta	Carpenter
Mynetere	Moneyer
Isensmið	Blacksmith
Baecestre	Baker
Scop	Story Teller

A list of food and drink that was required for King Ine and his court for one night has been kept on record, as follows:

Jars of Honey	10
Loaves	300
Casks of Welsh Ale	10
Casks of Clear Ale	30
Old Oxen	2
Geese	10
Hens	20
Cheeses	10
Cask of Butter	1
Salmon	5
Eels	100
Pounds of Fodder	20

Such items would have to be raised by the ealdorman being visited by the court. Kings traveled round to their subject estates making their presence felt and seeing that obligations were carried out such as repairs to roads, bridges, fortifications and military mobilization.

Saxon Months

Giuli Yule	First Month
Solmonatn	Month of cakes to the Gods
Hretha	Third
Eostre	Fourth
Thrimilci	Fifth Cows milked 3 times a day
Litha	Six and Seventh
Weod Monath	Eighth Month of Weeds
Maleg Monath	Holy Month Offerings End of Harvest
Winter Fylith	Tenth Month first Full Moon of winter
Blot Monath	Eleventh. Month of Sacrifice Killing Stock prior to Winter
Giuli	Last month

Saxon laws and Legal Terms

Athas and Ordelas	Oaths and Ordeals
Hamsochne	Home Breaking
Hundred Setena	Absence from the local Hundred Court
Morthas Murthers	Particularly Poison and Witchcraft
Forsteal	Assault
Flemenferth	Harboring a Fugitive
Burhbrice Borough-Breach	Burglary into Town Houses
Frithbrice	A breach of the Kings Peace
Girthbrice	A breach of the Local Peace